Spectral Realms

No. 22 ‡ Winter 2025

Edited by S. T. Joshi

> The spectral realms that thou canst see
> With eyes veil'd from the world and me.
>
> H. P. LOVECRAFT, "To a Dreamer"

SPECTRAL REALMS is published twice a year by Hippocampus Press,
P.O. Box 641, New York, NY 10156 (www.hippocampuspress.com).
Copyright © 2025 by Hippocampus Press.
All works are copyright © 2025 by their respective authors.
Cover artwork by Thorvald Niss (1842–1905), *The Drowned Man's
Ghost Tries to Claim a New Victim for the Sea*.
Cover design by Daniel V. Sauer
Hippocampus Press logo by Anastasia Damianakos.

ISBN 978-1-61498-465-8   ISSN 2333-4215

Contents

Poems 5
   Lost in a Dream / Ngo Binh Anh Khoa 7
   I Spoke the Incantations / Scott J. Couturier 8
   Heartbreak / Claire Smith 10
   Weird Sisters Three / Manuel Arenas 12
   Unpleasant Dreams / Geoffrey Reiter 14
   The Hands That Hold Me / Joshua Green 15
   Shell Shock: 2016 / Carl E. Reed 16
   Amongst the Shelves / Lee Clark Zumpe 20
   Beastly / Lori R. Lopez 22
   The Lyre of Lúca / Adam Bolivar 27
   Batrachian Prophets / Joshua Gage 28
   at the edge of the sea / Kurt Newton 29
   What Have You Done? / J. D. Dresner 30
   Through the Darkness Shines . . . / Michael Potts 31
   Last Cry unto the Night / Adam Amberden 32
   A Swigger's Saunter Down a Shunned Street / C. R. Molœny 34
   Charnel Mysteries / Katherine Kerestman 36
   Carcosan Shadows / Frank Coffman 37
   When Daylight Dies / Andrew White 38
   Credo / Manuel Pérez-Campos 39
   The Aberration / Joshua Green 40
   Due Diligence / DJ Tyrer 41
   The Night-Traveler, by Day, Keeps His Secrets / Silvatiicus Riddle ... 42
   In the Halls of the Dead / Ann K. Schwader 44
   Crimson Dawn / D. L. Myers 45
   Elemental Pact / William Clunie 46
   The Necromancer's Leman / David C. Kopaska-Merkel 48
   Progeny / David Barker 51
   Grave Bell / Scott J. Couturier 52
   Where the Shadows Bleed / Lee Clark Zumpe 53
   Casting Out / Ian Futter 54
   The Great Night / Adele Gardner 56

Night of the Sorcerers / Wade German 58
I Hear the Numbers / Maxwell I. Gold 60
Three Sonnets of the Weird / John Shirley 61
I Know There Is a Sunrise / Darrell Schweitzer 64
Ghosts / Kurt Newton 65
Committed in Sanity / Ngo Binh Anh Khoa 66
The Wells of the Weird: Ars Poetica / Carl E. Reed 71
Horror Home / Frank Coffman 72
The Blithebrook Fountain: A Folly / Steven Withrow 74
Five Full Moons / Jay Hardy 76
Ars Moriendi / Benjamin Blake 78
The Kingdom / Simon MacCulloch 79
Ratatoskr / Christian Dickinson 80
ghosts in trees / Lori R. Lopez 81
To Haunt Ancestral Tombs / Adam Bolivar 84
Fogs of Judgment / Janice Klain 86
Through Sunset's Gates / David Barker 87
Young Friend / William Clunie 88
Arkham Boys' Summer Afternoon / David C. Kopaska-Merkel 89
Fade / Lee Clark Zumpe 90
Cosmic Mind / Ron L. Johnson II 91
Bedeviled Kiss / Ashley Dioses 92
Eager Pupil / Katherine Kerestman 94
A Colossus in Dream / Maxwell I. Gold 95
Emperor Julian in the Afterworld / Darrell Schweitzer 96
Among the Trees / F. J. Bergmann 97
What They Say / Ngo Binh Anh Khoa 98
Hypercathexis to a Sunken Spell / Manuel Pérez-Campos 100
Walker of Wastes / Scott J. Couturier 102
In a Garden of Hounds / Benjamin Blake 104
On the Himalayas of Nicholas Roerich's Series of Paintings /
    Manuel Pérez-Campos 105

Classic Reprints 107
  Midnight / Archibald Lampman 109
  Adam to Lilith / E. Hoffmann Price 110
Reviews 111
  Fireside Poems / Kyla Lee Ward 113
  Halloween Redux / S. T. Joshi 115
Notes on Contributors 118

Poems

Lost in a Dream

Ngo Binh Anh Khoa

Each night I'd find myself a lost soul in
A strange, distorted wood that I was certain
Was but a dream, enshrouded in a curtain
Of shifting mist that seemed alive therein.
The moon glowed midst the starless sky, whose light
Stabbed the contorted, gale-whipped trees that shivered
And shed red sap amid the black and silver
Labyrinth in which I'd without fail catch sight
Of a tall figure stalking from afar,
But with each dream, that lurker shuffled nearer,
Its rotten odor and vile features clearer
With glaring eyes splattered on flesh of tar.
And in my last dream I came face to face
With it, my soul transformed in its embrace—
A new cursed tree trapped in its hellish space.

I Spoke the Incantations

Scott J. Couturier

(for Sam Raimi)

I have found the Necronomicon
In the cabin in the woods
Just past Elk Rapids.

I spoke the incantations,
Rousing the Kandarian Demon
From depths of some nether Abyss—

Now, powers unspeakable stir
In forest restless with inhabiting evil,
All hopes of escape hinging on oblivion.

For I have read of that foul text—
Desecrated my eyes, seared my soul,
& found a hideous resonance within.

Groans come from the fruit cellar—
A reel-to-reel tape plays tremulous invocations
To mirror my own fevered chanting—

I have found the *Necronomicon*
In the cabin in the woods
Just past Elk Rapids.

I spoke the incantations.

Note to this poem: The *Ash vs. Evil Dead* television series specifies that the cabin in the woods featured in the *Evil Dead* films is located just outside Elk Rapids, Michigan. As I grew up in northern Michigan, this is practically my backyard.

Heartbreak

Claire Smith

The shocks near killed me. I was rushed to hospital.
Blue lights blinked as I sunk into unconsciousness;
drowned in a well of the forgotten, like the princess's

gold ball. They had hauled me out of the deep. Nurses
told me surgeons had opened my chest, inserted
a pacemaker to electric shock back my broken heart—

my best friend was turned to a frog. A stranger's twisted
anger cursed him into an amphibian's body; he'd spurred
her, as if a fuse ticked, hissed, exploded and all at once

he was gone. As teenagers we had shared our secrets
huddled round camp fires, whispered by whispering
flames of the girls we'd first kissed, the girls we'd lost.

We'd tied so many knots together; tied up shared
memories. On winter's chill grass carpets, we kicked
a football about the school playing field—I always

let him win—happy enough not to argue the toss.
Summer days we lounged by a stream, picnicked
with cold sausages, soggy sandwiches, and squash

sipped from plastic bottles, like the best wine.
Woodland leaves gave us cheek-wet kisses in rain showers
soothed our bare backs from the smacks of the heat.

He'd spotted her playing throw and catch among the trees
the girl who would see through his frog's body, see his worth,
remodel him in her embrace. The shock of his familiar face
                              near killed me.

Weird Sisters Three

Manuel Arenas

As the gloam encroaches o'er the weathered battlements of Castle Dracula, snuffing the residual daylight like a douter, the Weird Sisters Three, bestirred, arise from their narrow beds within the crumbling cobwebbed crypt. Forthwith they repair to their eerie boudoir, whereupon they discover the boon the Count had left behind for their amusement before embarking for England has absconded during their diurnal dormancy. The sisters scour the dilapidated rooms of the castle in a frenzy searching for the runagate, alas, to no avail. *Dracula's guest* has fled and they are left bereft of their plaything.

    In high dudgeon, they descend upon the village for redress: flowing locks and tattered cerements fluttering like the wings of benighted fairies, their lissome figures floating above the forest floor, casting no shadow by the light of the moon as they flit from one casuta to another in search of a sanguinary repast. Their entrance repelled only from doorways adorned with garlic, hawthorn, and holy relics. Woe betide the household found by this infernal trio without these apotropaic wards. For none may otherwise escape the clutches of these harpies; all are fair game for their insatiable bloodlust.

    This eldritch trio presents a sinister sight to the hapless wayfarer: gold-tressed Flavia—comely in her countenance and favored by the Count—flanked by Lacramioara and Madalina, both of whom bear the aquiline profile of Dracula. Their jetty locks, sleek and black as a starless night, fall upon marmoreal shoulders like a pall. Rubicund eyes glower like balefires on their alabastrine faces, graced with sanguine lips that part in baleful smiles to reveal cuspidate teeth for rending throats. Their cries and laughter sound as knells to whomsoever has the misfortune to hear them.

The unfortunate auditors on this fell eventide are as follows: a strapping youth for ravishing Flavia, whose aureate mien and bewitching charms prove irresistible to any red-blooded man. A guileless maid for adroit Madalina, whose glamour and silver tongue lure the lass from her nightly devotions. And lastly, a mewling babe for Lacramioara, snatched from her bassinet whilst her callow mother answered the call of nature.

Returning to the crypt with the evening's spoils, the fell femmes indulge in a sanguinary orgy of demoniac proportions. The cries and supplications of their bedeviled victims are heard only by visitors from blood-soaked sprees of yore. Satiated for the nonce, they withdraw at the cockcrow to their soil-lined sarcophagi, where they lie in the torpor of the undead, dreaming of bats, bloodshed, and malefice to undertake upon their acronical revivication.

Unpleasant Dreams

Geoffrey Reiter

Chant me no soothing songs of tranquil rest
Within the bosom of my mother Earth,
The folding of my features into firth
And fen, for when my blood and bone are pressed
Into the soil and sod of her dry breast,
What mind of mine remains, what wealth of worth?
The dust that rushed into frail flesh at birth
Reclaims the thoughts that make me, unimpressed.

So if I'm laid in dirt where corpses, copses,
Collapse into organic matter, Why—?
Why should I not lament and vent my fury?
Cold comfort all these solemn thanatopses
That preach me peace and oneness when I die
If my sweet sentient self is what they bury.

The Hands That Hold Me

Joshua Green

I live alone within a house of hands,
Arms outstretched from the Hall of Those Before.
They grasp me as I feel the sacred glands,
Of a house that keeps her dead—evermore.
And in this house of hands that I abhor,
I let the ancients touch my living skin.
They say, "Now for us you live. Let us store
The sins we've passed from kin to kin to kin."
But I ignore and hear an older din—
The very first of me to ever breathe.
I hold his hand and tell him every sin
And let his nails dig in like poisoned teeth.

He tells me of a time before all pain,
As his infection spreads into my vein.

Shell Shock: 2016

Carl E. Reed

> He thrusts his fists against the posts
> and still insists he sees the ghost.
> —talismanic tongue-twister;
> or, the curse of Alpha Btry., 1st Bn., 11th Marines

In the years 2016 and 2017 the United States implemented a rather novel strategy to minimize casualties while battling the Islamic State in Syria. Instead of engaging the enemy with typical rifle platoon tactics—fire and maneuver, followed by an assault to close with and destroy the enemy—the Marine Corps and U.S. Army decided to attrit the foe by hurling tens of thousands of large-caliber shells at designated base camps and supply lines. Marines and soldiers in the batteries tasked with carrying out these missions were subjected, for days on end, to violent concussive blasts that hammered their internal organs, bones and flesh. Synapses in the brain misfired as dendritic connections broke down and energy-producing mitochondria died off. Returning veterans complained of a host of baffling maladies: delusions, paranoia, hallucinations. Some reported being haunted by ghosts, others of being stalked by nightmarish creatures out of a Hieronymus Bosch painting. One marine reported a black demon that hovered above his bed, another broke into a house after a psychotic break with reality to murder the person living there. When police arrived at the crime scene the marine asked them, "Are you going to take me to the moon now?" In ensuing months dozens of suicides followed. The Pentagon confesses confusion and dismay at this phenomenon while promising to look into the matter, even as they continue to discharge "problem" veterans into a life of homelessness and despair devoid of cushioning psychiatric and medical benefits. (For more details see "A Secret War, Strange New Wounds and Silence From the Pentagon," *New York Times*, 5 November 2023.)

The ghost was white as powdered bone
covered in chalky dust
eye sockets black as the Tartarean pit—
a thin wisp of a girl
naked, dress blasted off
by the 155mm shell
fired by the "triple seven" howitzer
(ten miles away)
that exploded at her feet
atomizing Zia & eight others
at point of impact:
Flash-boom! Oblivion.

Zia had returned
(I knew not how or why that name)
to my N.C.O. barrack's room
once again materializing
out of the wall locker
covered with posters of naked women,
motorcycles, hand guns & assault rifles.
The suffocating air:

sickly sweet
with the odors of shoe polish, Cosmoline
Brasso
& burnt flesh.

The girl shivered like a new-born faun
dumped steaming to the ground
slick with her mother's placental juices,
just now staggered erect for the first time
in some dispiriting dark forest
cold, alien & suffocating
as nightmare.
The screech of owls; screams of prey
torn apart
afar off, unseen
'midst arthritic tree limbs forked
into the unblinking red eye
of an o'er-watching autumnal moon.
Piercing thorns—
choking vines—
shifting loam amoeboid & pulsing
with charnel house energy.
Chaos. Anti-life.

"Go! Leave me be!

I did my duty.
I fired as ordered
at grid coordinates
on a map."

I know
says the girl
you did not mean to kill me.
One hand to her lips, the other
pointing at my chest.
(The universe is tilting, tilting, tilting . . .)
but
(Vertigo! Everything has crashed into something else.)
you did.

Moan
ghost
driven from
the Earth.

Amongst the Shelves

Lee Clark Zumpe

One might, upon a cold and dismal afternoon—
a mist of rain dully descending
from the lowering gray sky—
take refuge in some curious sanctuary

such as a nameless secondhand bookshop
    found in a forgotten alleyway
    crowded with writhing shadows
and an anarchy of residual memories.

One would, sensing a pervasive dissonance—
    the friction of unuttered blasphemies
    perched on the lips of the elderly proprietor—
hesitate to move beyond the outer threshold

and bear whatever expense might be incurred
    by lingering, even fleetingly,
    amongst the cobwebbed shelves
of the antiquarian's labyrinthine ossuary.
One can, through uncanny enticements and persuasions—
    by whispered promises of arcane lore
    and calls to conquer unimaginable vistas—
become beguiled into momentary submission,

drifting unknowingly into boundless shadows,
    yielding to disembodied voices
    reverberating through time and space,
afflicting the most desperate of infirmities.

Beastly

Lori R. Lopez

Vast and uncharted lies the wicked deep,
a mysterious realm with no laws to keep,
except that a bigger maw than your own
could gulp you down. Don't swim alone!

A beastly kiss will await them what do,
and I'll not leak a tear for the unwary few
who fail to abide by this singular pact—
beware a damsel whose heart is cracked!

She travels transparent as particles of wet;
a trail of bubbles—ill tides of Babette.
Mustn't let her surround yer body or soul.
Babette can swallow a whaler whole!

Nary salt can calm the monsoon of fears!
She'll rise in a spray or cascade in tears,
her molecules streaming like gray pallid orbs
after countless vessels that she absorbs.

Pursuing a fleet or a single stray urn,
Babette may bite off the bow or stern
and gobble that bucket of malicious stew,
teeth gnashin' from anger at evils men do!

A vengeful angel against the worst deeds.
For the victims of wanton and wasteful greeds,
who are oft the most gentle monsters at sea.
An appetite for ships that slaughter the free!

Babette was a woman drowned by a cap'n—
dumped in the ocean to silence her yappin'
to spare the great creatures that he disdained.
In a vault of iron and still she complained!

Lashed by thick chains; heaved o'er the side . . .
descended to the bottom where bones abide.
Yet her spirit was strong—her soul unbound!
In that lonely grave she would not be found.

Rottenborn sounded a most fitting name
on a man who harbored no drop of shame,
and sold his mother to the largest bidder
fer becomin' a burden: a sobbing widder!

Babette he had won while cheatin' at dice,
pledged by a barkeep, a very low price
to be rid of a daughter who acted the boss,
his eyes well-closed in that fateful toss.

A skipper with naught than a yen for possession,
like others who chase a phantom obsession,
creating the ghosts of their beastliest foes—
he carried the wench for his Compass Rose.

Her likeness sculpted to guide the prow . . .
Captain Rottenborn sliced the spar with a vow:
"Let the fathoms embrace ye, tongue and spirit!
Scream all ye wish! May the Devil hear it!"

Sheathing a cutlass, he strode to the deck
and laughed quite merrily, a weight off his neck—
chillin' the depths with her cold dead touch,
as doomed as the beasts she loved so much!

Three masts would creak, their sails full-wind.
The *Grim Tide* coursed and voices dinned
upon her bridge, guzzlin' rum and jigging
while the captain clung to rail or rigging.

She must be gone. He could breathe a sigh,
for that barmaid cursed the waves too high.
Kegs too brackish. Waters seemed barren.
The canvases slack. A red eye above glarin'.

Rotten had blamed these random mishaps
and punished her wrongs with stunning slaps,
till the lass was determined to collect her due
on the craft and its wretched murderous crew!

He suspected she cut his nets to haul prey,
even sabotaged boats to wash away—
after tossin' harpoons and gear overboard—
so he locked her where the catch was stored.

'Midst barrels of sundried fish and squid;
among casks of oil the brute kept her hid,
then sank her cage at a forsaken spot . . .
an uncharted point the stars knew not—

Of woebegone fates for brash females—
like caterwaul torrents of cat-o'-nine-tails
that deal retribution, deliver harsh flails
with a force or fury, a tempest of nails.

If blood the fiend sought, so in kind she'd pay,
through a flood of brine and a storm of spray—
pure vigor concentrated; a maelstrom's birth,
gathering dimensions of breadth and girth . . .

This crusading ghost—an orca's salvation;
savior of humpbacks, the entire whale nation;
engulfing vile ships, crushed by her smile—
fattening the beasts loathed by Rotten a while!

She caused the *Grim Tide* to be taken aback:
halting so quick the masts lay in a stack—
meeting an iron wall of aquatic wrath—
keeling and splitting, a wraith's aftermath!

Captain Rotten she cast to the darkest trench
where a body would bloat; skin must blench,
confined to a dungeon constructed of bones:
the ribs of the giants whose lives none owns.

The Lyre of Lúca

Adam Bolivar

Shadows caper   as the scopmaid sings,
Her long fingers   lingering subtly
On stretched catgut,   stirring sorrow.
Black her lyre is,   blighted in legend,
Crafted by Lúca   from cursed hazel,
Strings enchanted   with stolen mead,
Bless'd, blood-wetted   by a bonfire's glow.
In darkness dwells   the doomed maiden,
Endless her journey   under moonlight,
In halls singing   hoary ballads
Of Géac Yoresung.   Yonder she seeks him,
Tireless her yearning   for the tricksy youth,
A wyrd woven   by wicked sisters,
Cackling madly,   carving runestaves.

[Note: Lúca is an Old English cognate of Loki. Géac—a speculative Old English rendering of Jack—is pronounced 'yawk.']

Batrachian Prophets

Joshua Gage

dedicated to Frank Coffman

flood wreckage—
this anthropodermic tome
glistens undamaged

moldy catacombs—
translating pictograms
writ in human blood

our webbed hands
scraping back the mud . . .
the veined membrane
cradling green yolks
and generations of pain

freezing rain . . .
star by star, our children croak
the sky to flames

at the edge of the sea

Kurt Newton

at the edge of the sea
where the ghost ships land
and dead fingers reach
from out of the deep

at the edge of the sea
where the salt meets the sand
fall the tears widows weep
binding water with blood

at the edge of the sea
come the lost and the grieved
the waves fill their lungs
with a sorrowful song

at the edge of the sea
from out of the foam
in a tangle of weeds
the tide brings the bones

What Have You Done?

J. D. Dresner

      You stole from me.
I was once lonely, uncertain, jaded
then you whisked that all away without asking, you thief in the night.

      You scared me.
Standing over the unknown abyss, taking my hand,
assuring me we would fly, daring me to leap alongside you.

      You possessed me.
Interlocking my soul with yours like a voodoo marionette,
for when I laugh, you laugh—when I cry, you cry.

      You ruined me.
With your love, your energy, your beauty;
my palate has become spoiled. I'll never yearn for anything less.

Through the Darkness Shines . . .

Michael Potts

Your mind a labyrinth of delightful
Horror, caught in eldritch realms
Of gloom, haunted by Barnabas
Collins' ghostly bites, remnants
of past haunts on a set prone
to blunder and brilliance.

A disco queen figure shaped
In the dark of a bar by glow
Of flashing lights and dance
Moves that would turn me
Inside out. So lost you are!

Faith rejected, replaced
By a Lovecraftian world,
Azathoth's mad dash through
A universe insane, meaning,
Non-being, and being, lack
Of meaning, yet strangely

belief in truth, beauty,
goodness persists, an existential
thrusting of a personal sword
striving to slice through dark.

Last Cry unto the Night

Adam Amberden

A wolf alone, pack fled ages past
Adrift in a dying land
Echoes of their wild songs fading fast
Spittle and blood
    where once was voice
Bitter effluent of a battered heart

A tear, freshly wept
Mud in the ashen hollow
Where fitfully slept
The ragged beast
    of rasping breath,
of failing limb, so close to . . .

Bolt awake to a familiar call
Stoking the embers of hope
Compelling his manic search and fall.
Just wind howling
    through ghosts of trees
No pack to find, but he tried

The Shadows come
    dancing to a wicked,
        unheard tune.

Just as sickly peace fills his home,
Silver streaks of light
Pierce the tenebrous violet gloam.
Pearlescent hands part the veil;
    She emerges
Clad in golden, gossamer gown.

She approaches with grace supernal,
Raises him up to stand as a man
His pelt of pain drops down, filth and all
Freed of his cage,
    He watches himself go
New verdant growth fills his eyes.

For a moment,
    the wolf stood,
        lurched forward . . .
Then, without a sound,
    he laid down,
        and he died.
A tear, freshly wept
Diamond on the ground.

A Swigger's Saunter Down a Shunned Street

C. R. Molœny

In midnight dreary
With cloying obumbrates flowing in queery
And the tidal shroud acting in masque, hideously,
Stalks a man darkly,
White skin shadowed from the Night's fumes, sorely—
Saunters he in daunting and unabiding mists staggeredly,
Gripping his waist-pocket niggardly,
Reaching for his drinking flask sluggardly,
Nearing it towards his crusty lips shakedly . . .
But then! a shape blackly
Dashes 'cross his crapulous vision horrifically!
In a monstrous gallop.

O but where is he? . . .
But upon the stricken, oozing pavements of Merber Lane,
Placard scratched evilly to write: MURDER LANE!
A drunkard's mosey befoulled
Accursed doom-deridden swoosing
What foolishly-choiced boozing!
Upon a night so satanically looming . . .
And then—
From the chain-wired fence
Comes a terrific strain of sunderance,

Of metal bursting
And steel tearing—
And heaves therein rufescent mists
With deadly character!
And the night drinker,
The heavy swiller,
The odious swigger!
Lags backward
For emerges therefrom
A jagged hulk
A furrysome bulk
And upon its hind-legs comes a stalk
And fangs gnarled shown for jaw unlockt
And nails long and whorled and black
And sinews athrob in this beastly beefcake.

For thrills pursu'd
Threshings issu'd,
For ravacity lewd
Monstrous vibrations cu'd,
And amidst flesh torn, smithereen'd,
Puddles ethyl alcohol C_2H_5OH.

Charnel Mysteries

Katherine Kerestman

Tomb secrets lie in wait in cold compartments buried deep,
Whispering truths, enigmas, lies, deceit, mysteries, lore
In charnel dialects and unearthly grammars, hissed
Through sutured lips and gelatinous tongues and gums,
Summoning unholy needs and exciting gruesome lusts
In aerial things flapping rubbery wings that roil
Putrid night mists into tunnels not unlike the funnel
Of the maelstrom into which tall masted ships descend
To glimpse the squirming abysses of oblivion,
Fall into illimitable chasms, whence ghastly
Night-things crawl to listen with their ears to the gravestones,
Hearkening to the loathsome incantations they utter.

Carcosan Shadows

Frank Coffman

Once every thousand years Carcosa's thirteen moons,
Each one at full, reflecting the Twin Sunlight,
Into an awesome pattern themselves arrange—
The Conlunation of the Yellow Sign. Eftsoons,
When that dread dual daylight breaks weird Night,
The Shadows lengthen in a way most strange.

For close—but separate—Twin Suns array;
The Black Stars flee before those infernal Eyes;
The moons, in cluster, set beyond the rim;
Blended penumbrae announce Insanity's Day,
(Each caught in blackest umbra quickly dies—
If not already dead!) Then—all grows dim . . .

As the Black Sun eclipses full the Red,
And the Yellow King comes forth with silent tread.

When Daylight Dies

Andrew White

There's magic in the midnight moon,
So much more than sunny noon.
Shadows dance and ghosts abound,
Night birds make a stirring sound.

Something happens in the soul
When the sky is black as coal.
Underneath the lunar light,
Ancient powers reach their height!

So come with me when night is here,
Together we can have no fear.
We dance until the darkness ends—
When daylight dies, I meet my friends.

Inspired by Annie Stegg Gerard's painting *The Forest Procession*.

Credo

Manuel Pérez-Campos

I sing of bards who can rememorate in black hole
lines a trillion-sunned lore and of the wind
elementals who insert outsider distances under
their feet: who can hold like a talisman in the hollow
of the hand without having it burnt through
a shard from an epoch's monolithic darkness:
and whose every mused utterance is like a luminous,
parsimonious theorem, a lever to move the earth
away from that builder of great never-afters,
a sunlight-blocking timestorm in the immemorial
void: whose vision when prophesying in this cramped,
overcrowded galaxy becomes elastic to accommodate
new arisings: and who keep transitioning between
their two favorite shapes, dead and undead, with
a sparrow older than the pyramids on the shoulder: for
lo: they are the avatars of what humankind could be.

The Aberration

Joshua Green

Upon the waves of Lake Superior
There sits an island drained of humankind.
For what lurks there is not inferior
To those that cannot grasp the sea-gull's mind.

Her eyes are scarlet and wide, ill designed.
She sees what we cannot—a depthless lake.
She hears the things below that stripped the rind
Of pagan ships that fell within their quake.

In time the aberration cries, waves break
Upon the island's shores. The sea-gull's tongue
Then speaks the words that calls the gods to wake
To feast upon metal—humankind's red young.

And when they come they rise with mossy teeth,
To eat the ships and bring them underneath.

Due Diligence

DJ Tyrer

Due diligence means you ought to persist
Continuing with this case is a must
Even as you bleed the last of your trust
At yet another deceitful twist
Strike another name off your list
As into growing madness you are thrust
And honeyed words fill your heart with lust
For a girl you know does not exist

Homicide piled upon homicide
Bodies posed in macabre display
Your skills those tableaux seem to deride
Mocking you both night and day
The truth is not yours to decide
But what is written in the play

The Night-Traveler, by Day, Keeps His Secrets

Silvatiicus Riddle

Fruitless, does the dreamer by daylight
not grasp at thought-clouds
as they escape through windows,
mouse-holes, and wall cracks?

Well, then I grasp at the fleeting stuffs.

Could I decipher the dregs of dreams?
Upturn the remains onto the chipped porcelain
pages of a diary—each esoteric word like mountain mist
hanging on a beam of light?

I scratch out the strange sygils in black pen,
and smear the ink in haze and in haste:

toad skull, black cat, dove-in-flight,
dung beetle, candle wax, coded light,
a moon that burns holes
in the black film of night,
a smile returned, a golden key,
quicksilver drops—a count of three,
the glaring eyes of an all-hallow's kite,
a prick of each thumb to attain second sight

It leaves me now.
The night-traveler, by day, keeps his secrets,
and thus, the unknown draws back unto itself—
dark threads coiled upon spools of moonlight,
and tucked away on the high shelves of the heart.

I ask the morning sun:
what becomes of dreams, faded and forgotten,
at the apex of waking?

The words come warmly, in birdsong,
and in the sharp crack of frost:
What is enigma to the mind
but legend to the soul?

In the Halls of the Dead

Ann K. Schwader

In the halls of the dead, all conversations
may be resumed. No clocks intrude
upon this breathless endless quiet
twilight. Nothing cracks the mood

of contemplation decades deep
& clear as mirrors set to trap
a shadow half remembered. Words
keep their own counsel here. Perhaps

you did the same—for far too long,
until the taste of ashes fell
across your tongue like winter. Stayed
through springs you had so much to tell

to no one left. No seasons, here:
no ashes, snow, or petals drift
across these floors worn dull with need
& indecision. Time's a gift

that gives past bearing. Given back,
it lightens up the tongue once more
discussing nothing, everything
at once behind a fading door.

Crimson Dawn

D. L. Myers

In the crimson dawn, on a blood-red sea,
Where the shadows die, and the dead are free,
And the moonlight flees in the growing light,
While the mainsail sings in the fleeing night.

Dark the waters churn in that sanguine deep
Where the currents stream and the Kraken sleep,
And the icy depths of that boundless black
Hold the vessels lost that the demons wrack.

Now the vultures turn in a bleeding sky,
And the deck's awash in a burning lye,
And from out the grasp of those scourging waves,
All the dark souls rise that no sermon saves.

Elemental Pact

William Clunie

'Twas a slipshod happenstance, our dark enlightenment,
that night we learned that we could kill with simple
ritual, no more a bother than the bending of a spoon.

Mister Wister fell down stairs and troubled Jimmy
nevermore. Then we turned to mine own foe:
Mrs. Scissors smacked my hand in trigonometry
for telling her I had no use for such dull art
when I did see this world in holy geomancy.
Well for that she had to die. The tram of life
she leapt before is one that comes for all of us,
but timing—well, it's everything. This time was ours,
we all got rich, famous even, one of us, but then
it had to come, the falling out, as fallouts will:
the demons of the demiurge do not like to share;
they have their own agendas. So the others had to die.

I proved quite skilled at games of trickery and blood.
Curtis died in mud that clutched him as he walked,
dirt to dirt that filthy cuss, and Jimmy—James now—
felt the little tongues of flame inside his precious
burning library. Earth and Fire, yes indeed, now only Air
for Alistair, as I follow up this flight of stairs, behind him
as he steps out on the battlement to overlook the bricolage
of his estate below, that silly moat he had to have, I'm leaning

out beyond the stone, drawn to it with some odd need,
the smooth enticing Water at my reach, my arm outstretched,
forgotten now why I am here, and then a little beast
that rides on Air pushes at the gentle fulcrum of my spine—

as I fall down I find the terror of the pact we formed
made manifest with eyes inside the water gleaming,
and familiar maws of avarice that widen now, to speak,
to whisper words that have no meaning, inhuman
voices that engulf us as we drown.

The Necromancer's Leman

David C. Kopaska-Merkel

The basement pool,
its limpid fluid
rippled nervously
with every passing train,
gaslit from sconces
spaced around the stony walls,
it seemed to plumb
an unimaginable abyss.

Lynx-like she padded
to the pool's lip;
naked, she slipped in,
crimson and auric robe
shed carelessly on the tiles;
her body, swiftly swimming,
shrank, faded from view,
not a bubble nor ripple
disturbed the pool's surface.

Far above, dark doings
in the lab; foul stenches,
excruciated sounds;
her master strove to
wrench secrets from the dead;

the moon's skull drew clouds
across its argent face.

The lamia's head broke
the surface, her eyes,
alabaster disks,
reflected nothing;
otter-like, she leapt
from the pool,
drew on her silken robe.

Lithely she climbed
the subterranean stair,
emerging behind a giant
statue that squatted,
four-armed and scowling,
wing tips far above its head.
She crossed to the broad
stair that led to the master's lab,
continued silently to its door.

She pushed it open a crack
and entered: "Leave me,"
he barked, not turning;
carefully added vermilion drops
to a bubbling alembic.

Not hearing the door close,
he began to turn; she was
right there, nude and glistening,
hands reaching for his head,
jaws unhinged; he screamed,
briefly.

The lab, moon-flooded,
was silent now, the necromancer,
supine and white;
the lamia licked crimson
lips, ablaze in lunar glory.

Progeny

David Barker

Avoid the road that runs along the cliff,
They said, when walking to the town of Zoar.
A witch tore up that path—now it's no more
Than rutted dirt, above where ship wrecks drift.
Ignoring this, I took the high road, soon
Came to a mossy house on rock set high
Where it was lashed by winds that moan and sigh,
And in the sky, a glowing, gibbous moon.

About to turn and leave, I heard a cry—
An awful blend of grief and rage insane
And glimpsed a deformed face with swollen eye
That leered at me through attic windowpane.
I fled in fear, escaped that dreadful scene:
Part man, part rat: O deviant obscene!

Inspired by H. P. Lovecraft's sonnet "XII. The Howler" in *Fungi from Yuggoth*.

Grave Bell

Scott J. Couturier

Ah! How hideous it is to all human sense:
Hearing the ringing of that bleak grave bell.
Buried with he whose loss is beyond recompense:
Left to sound should he wake in coffin's cell.

You may wonder why I do not cry out for joy:
Why I fetch no lantern, nor reach for spade.
Instead I shudder, shunning gravedigger's employ:
& the bell so clear, clanging wild & mad!

Caution to question before concluding my tale:
Well might terror, as love, quicken one's pulse.
But no pulse has he, though the bell clangor & flail:
Interred for three months! Yet hear him convulse.

Rung always at nightfall, since a fortnight from his funeral:
I suspect in some dark hour this summons will call
& at last I shall answer, both Love & Death's thrall.

Where the Shadows Bleed

Lee Clark Zumpe

where darkness writhes
and horrors hide
in preternatural pools;

where phantoms gather
and Twilight glimmers
across her sparkling jewels;

where zealots labor
for some gods' favor
out of time and space;

where shadows bleed
beneath keen blades
the stars seem out of place.

Casting Out

Ian Futter

When the whole of time has emptied
and its carcass is picked clean,
you'll strain to hear my vacant voice
amongst the browning green.

When summer suns have shifted
to wan and wintry light,
you'll hark to hear dark laughter there
within the lengthening night.

For I'm tethered by this tombstone
and the symbols which you scrawled,
Believing that my banishment
was good for one and all.

You'd watched me weaving wonders
from the weft of withered gloom,
discerned my carved catastrophes,
which leapt within my loom,

And chased me through the wasted winds,
armed with your books and spells.
You hunted me into the depths
of hurtling, hungry hells.

You faced my forms to force me
to the fate that you had planned,
while many cowered beneath my glare
and trembled in their land.

Believing that my shifting shape
was better put to rest,
you chained me to this underworld,
within this writhing nest.

And now you dream in dullness
of your fortunes free from fear,
But I can hear those sleepy prayers,
which beg to bring me near.

The Great Night

Adele Gardner

It's almost Halloween. My mother climbs into the attic,
returning with metal-toothed orange noisemakers
painted with witches and cats; with tiny pumpkins just big enough
for a child's thimble; with wax candles of ghosts and black cats on fence
    posts.
I fall asleep each night with a warm black cat tucked under each arm,
father (Cory) and daughter (Rosa), listening to their tales of nighttime
    rambles,
adventures with the witch queen, and how they hope I'll join them.

My mother knows their secrets: purrs with them
by candlelight, turning their stories to living shadows on the wall,
her spell-soaked fingers drawing black cats
to guide lonely witches through the night.
She tells me, "You can always trust a black cat."
I share the secret of my heart: "I wish I were one."
"So do we," our black cats purr. I prowl with them at the witching hour,
memorize their lessons on how to ride a broom and navigate fear,
then snuggle close as I slip into my favorite dream: joining my black cat
    family.

At last, the great night arrives. Mom helps me step lively
into the furry black cat suit she made at my request,
sewn with love and stitched with spells.
While she plays the black-enameled music box she won from Death,
our black cats yowl along, and Mom's delicate fingers work their magic.

I twitch my whiskers, my tail, brush noses with Rosa, nuzzle Cory's
    cheek,
then nestle in one of Mom's arms, while Rosa rides her shoulder
and Cory perches high on the broom handle to guide us
as we sail into the night to place our silhouettes against the harvest
    moon.

Night of the Sorcerers

Wade German

The tribesmen say where primal jungles spread,
On full moon nights the sorcerers return
From realms reserved beyond for evil dead:

Upon such nights, the demon cauldrons churn
To overflow with mist that animates
Dark shadows, warping shape of tree and fern

To take on semblance of black temple gates
Where stranger darkness pulses, seems to breathe;
Where beasts retreat in silent, fearful hate

As creeping vines, like writhing vipers, weave
Around an idol ancient and abhorred,
That squats obscured by venom-bearing leaves—

A site where armoured corpses clutching swords
Arise from undergrowth-entangled graves,
Their necromantic order now restored:

They seek out human lives to claim as slaves,
Stealing a soul by force of binding spells;
And woe are they who hear the rising waves

Of spectral wailing out of unseen wells,
For earth to netherworld has been transposed
And shackled souls are dragged to dungeoned hells . . .

By dawn the gates are gone, by vines enclosed.

I Hear the Numbers

Maxwell I. Gold

Amid the stale twilight beneath a pallid darkness, I heard distant sirens howl, calling for the doom of flesh and consciousness. Soon a sour amber dawn aroused my deepest fears, while the cries from a billion pathetic souls wailed through the streets, the heat and hatred wrought by a thunderous artificial solution warmed my face. Illusions were contorted, though foolishly welcomed, by the terrible appearance of the Yellow Star whose barbarous musings slammed into the bedrock of innovation. The monuments to our unholy climb into the stars, cities and plastic men fell towards the waning, fiery mouths of a broken world like bone and glass shards.

    A tentacled sentience both monstrous and incorporeal, one after another like trillions of thorns ripped apart the once peaceful cerulean skies. Invisible and deadly was the beast's hunger like knives falling from the clouds, we were helpless to dodge the sharp cuts and cruel twists from an unrelenting force peeling back the poor fragile thoughts of a primitive and cruel race.

    Unable to succumb to the fat, bulbous pressures wrought by the dreadful weight of Ad'Naigon's sinister persistence, I felt the pathetic remnants of my body bend toward a state of demented bliss. Too late did I care for a release from my blood-soaked lips, and eyes pooled by mucus, and other heinous fluids; for the only relief where I finally understood, beyond a dark metallic chuckle—*I heard the numbers.*

Three Sonnets of the Weird

John Shirley

1.
He shares the crowded house that is my skull
The only guest who does not dissipate
The others fade as if a daydreamed trull
But he sojourns and always watching, waits
He nods and smiles when I lash out at you
With pleasure he rewards my worst instincts
He dizzies truth so falsehood seems more true
He covers up dark sources of the links
Not guest and not a stranger now is he
I've known him always and a fading night
From trauma nurtured I my enmity
Laughed bitterly when hope grayed from my sight

Then one hot night I breathe my final rasp
I see him use the doorway of my gasp

2.
Lost in a forest I was found at last
When I was farthest from the sight of men
The One who found me was the goddess Bast
She rose from silent waters of the fen

As when a tiger swims in rivers wild
Bast roared as she shook droplets into gems
She sang of Egypt and the crocodile
And yowling mourned the gods whom Man condemns

I know great God cannot this goddess spare
But find her eyes in jewels of lambent green
Her litheness ripples in the evening air
A forest is a temple to this queen

I knew I'd found the true source of the Nile
(Perhaps she'll let me live for just a while)

3.
In Cornwall folk describe a living mist
That clings to Daphne's storied Bodmin Moor
Where smugglers have their shadowed windblown tryst:
The mist restores to life those lost in war

And I perceive a living, fevered rust
With its red pen in steel engraving fate
(Rust thus inscribes our lives as living dust)
Tales told in tattered words are traced too late

A living wind sings shrill from Cornwall cliffs
Surf booms like cannon from the sunken ships
Cold waves with marbled, cursived foaming glyphs
Write names spoken from icy bearded lips

And poets drifting through the misty glen
Search endlessly for pencil or a pen

I Know There Is a Sunrise

Darrell Schweitzer

I know there is a sunrise
beyond that bleak, far shore.
So we heave the ferryman overboard,
hijack his boat,
and drift in silence,
past the shadowy islands,
where marble tombs gleam,
out of the mouth of the black river,
into that ocean that no chart has ever described,
beneath strange stars, then no stars at all,
beyond all the world's dreaming,
into the new dawn, the new day,
beyond all reach of gods and death.
I know it's around here somewhere.
In the dark.
Expectation.
In the dark.
Hope, faith.
The sea like black glass.
I know there is a sunrise.
The dark.
The sea.
The silence.

Ghosts

Kurt Newton

It seems like I'm the only one
drifting in between,
the others hardly notice me.
They hear the rattle of a door,
they see the flicker of a light,
they feel a coolness in the air.
But to them I'm nothing more
than the settling of the house,
a sudden draft, a faulty wire.
The spaces I once occupied
have filled in like the ocean tide.
I've vanished like the morning mist,
banished from the present
into a past that only now exists
in memories of before, never after.
But of this I can be sure:
only when it happens to them,
when their life has left its host,
will they truly believe in ghosts,
and then it will no longer matter.

Committed in Sanity

Ngo Binh Anh Khoa

It's said that there must be a reason why
One would bear hatred for one's fellow kind,
A learned behavior burned into one's mind
Or righteous wrath for suffered wrongs, but I
Can't think of any cause behind the spite
I felt toward my now bed-bound master, who
Was not long for this world, but for his cruel
And wolfish eyes, which tortured me with fright.
Those predatory things would haunt my thought
And stir in me the roiling urge to kill.
His glare, though greatly weakened, vexed me still
And prompted me to execute the plot
I'd with precision planned out just to make
Sure they would close and nevermore would wake.

For some weeks, I covertly got to work
And fanned the flame of turmoil in his head
With soft sounds in his chamber in the dead
Of night like those of specters in the murk.
I'd relish in his helplessness and see
His terror when he woke to alien sounds;
My faint light caught his eyes this time around,
And my hate, long suppressed, flared up when he
Raised his head, choked cries spilling from his lips,
Which softly rang within the thick walls where

The shroud of darkness plagued his frantic stare,
A cornered, stalked prey locked in Terror's grip.
I watched him weakly squirm a little more
And savored his groans wracked with pain and awe.

His baleful eyes were stark against the space
Submerged in blackness, each a dwindling dot
Suspended in my lantern's light and caught
In the Grim Reaper's sight. There was no place
To hide when Death's unseen scythe nearer loomed,
But Death was in no hurry, for the prey
Was trapped. The quickened breathing gave away
The old man's fear, for he knew he was doomed;
He yanked the bell pulls, but no servant came
While I stood still and listened to the noise
That madly beat beneath his fragile voice:
The sound of his own heart. My inner flame
Of rage was further stoked by its wild beats
Compelling me to forward move my feet.

His yell was silenced by my gloved hand ere
I shoved all of his sleeping pills inside
His throat, and as the old man slowly died,
I gazed into his wide eyes fraught with fear.
A gratifying grin spread on my face,

For I at last would purge the tyrant in
This manor. Though my hands were stained with sin,
My soul would be forgiven by God's grace.
His eyelids struggled to stay open while
His heartbeat thundered in my clouded head
Until it wavered, weakened, and went dead.
His eyes were shut. His heart was still. The trial
Was done. I checked the corpse. The pulse was gone.
I'd then conceal my track till break of dawn.

The emptied bottle of pills was placed in
His hand. I then removed my prints where they
Would raise suspicion, took the gloves away,
And fixed the tampered service bells within
The slumbering manor, tying up loose ends
Before returning to my room to wait
For his cold body to be found. So great
Was the relief that I could breathe again.
I took a well-earned nap before a scream
Of some poor maid tore through the quietude
And roused the house into a hectic mood
As all the servants scrambled to the scene,
Where I became a voice among the choir,
A spark that helped to spread the frenzied fire.

A shout for order suddenly soared and broke
Through the cacophony. The clamor died.
Some called the cops while others stayed inside
To keep the site unaltered. By some stroke
Of luck, they placed me at the open door,
Which gave me more time to rehearse my tale
Before the officers came, and all was hale;
I'd play my role. I'd weep and whimper for
The audience till the show concluded, and
I'd leave this place and start anew somewhere,
Free from the memory and that terrible glare,
A whole new chapter for a whole new man.
But as the reverie blossomed in my head,
I heard a sound that I had thought was dead!

It started as a low and dull noise in
The air, but as the seconds passed, it'd grow
Much louder, nearer, exponentially so;
Its rhythmic beats would ricochet within
My eardrums till I could not hear my thought.
Those horrid beats prowled on me like wild beasts
And madly ravaged my mind without cease.
In my peripheral vision then, I caught
Sight of a movement, one that could not be!
The old man was a corpse! His eyes were closed!

I'd sealed those damn things! They were not supposed
To open anymore! But there, I'd see
Those hateful orbs of sickening blue. They stared,
Unblinking, binding me in their cruel snare!

I lashed out as the summoned officers came
And roughly pinned me down, their harsh words drowned
By those unholy beats! Those wretched sounds!
I shrieked, abandoning all restraint and shame!
"I killed you, villain!" I heard myself cry,
My hoarse voice warring with the deafening beats
As I, in vain, sprang up, "I did the deed!
Stop glaring at me with your evil eyes!"
Oh, how I wished to rip them out, along
With that bedeviling heart that would not stop!
Oh, how I yearned to seize them both and chop
Them into bits! The beats, though, grew too strong!
Defeated, I did one last thing deemed smart:
I begged to be jailed and kept far apart
From that cursed glare and hideous beating heart!

The Wells of the Weird: Ars Poetica

Carl E. Reed

The wells of the weird are sunk in flesh
drilling down, down to primordial depths:

the Great Mother & the Shadow, the Tree of Life,
bright fiery phoenix & the blood-drenched knife.

The wind-daggered moor on a dark, moonless night;
hushed sylvan grotto fairy-folk'd at twilight.

Entirety of cosmos, nullity of void;
All that is created—all that is destroyed.

Ensorcel, poet! Evoke in words.
Thou art mystic, seer & fraught demiurge.

Horror Home

Frank Coffman

A darkness deep descends at dusk
Here in this house, a hollow husk
Of what was once a happy home,
A place where merry days would come. . . .
But then came *Death*. The curtains drawn.
Now lair of ghosts, the living gone.
 How could they know they'd come to dwell
Above one of the Gates to Hell?
But hark! Through dark before the dawn,
Phantoms hold sway, and demon spawn
Infest this place—feed on the pain
Residing here. Foul deaths again
And yet again—murders most foul
Replay each night. The victims howl
In agony. The killer's blade
Stabs again into ghost-wounds made
That fatal night so long ago.

And in the village far below
That hilltop house, all people know
To shun the place. Most dare not go
E'en near that hill. For legends say
Those few who've dared have died the day
They tempted fate and tamed their fears.
Thus, none alive for many years

Have roamed the halls of that cursed home.
All heed the legend: "None have come
Back from that Hell-house on the hill.
Their *bodies rot, souls dwell there still!*
They've swelled the number of *The Lost*
And now howl with that horrid host."

The Blithebrook Fountain: A Folly

Steven Withrow

Within the public garden,
A constant haunt of mine,
There is a sprawling fountain
Of such grotesque design,
The feeling is malign.

The marble, if it's marble,
From which the fountain's made
Has oxidized to yellow,
And even in the shade,
Its jaundice doesn't fade.

Speaking of how the stonework
Assaults surrounding space
Would discompose a poet—
A sculptural disgrace
One's mind will not erase.

Goat-girls, ape-owls, erupting
At angles too obtuse,
In matters geometric,
To be of any use;
They are their own excuse.

And then there is the water
That spurts like juice from jet
To jet, while hissing geysers
Suffuse the air with wet,
And I cannot forget

Those queer and shifting patterns
Of liquid shot across
That crack-skulled mason's basin
No sane man would emboss;
It leaves me at a loss.

Yet still the public garden,
It calls me to account
For crimes I'm unaware of;
It *dares* me to surmount
That fierce, disfigured fount!

Five Full Moons

Jay Hardy

First full moon:
A little change.
She does feel
Slightly strange.
Her head hurts.
It's suddenly sore.
She stops by
The drug store.

Second full moon:
A little worse.
But nothing like
The monthly curse.
Her eyes ache.
They're rather red.
She sleeps late
In her bed.
Third full moon:
A little hair.
Peculiar patches
Here and there.
Her skin burns.
It's horribly hot.
She applies lotion.
All she's got.

Fourth full moon:
A little howl.
Followed by
A guttural growl.
Hands and feet
Practically paws.
She pedicures
Her new claws.

Fifth full moon:
A little scary.
Head to toe
Completely hairy.
Her body feels
Remarkably right.
She goes out
For a bite.

Ars Moriendi

Benjamin Blake

These angels and demons
Vie for final claim
Over this tired soul.
Can the dried blood be washed from the cup of charity?
Can these brittle bones hold up to the strain,
With so many self-inflicted fractures to boast?
I laid down my arms
Only to use my trembling hands,
And I am at a loss
For truly knowing
What side it is that I am on,
As the final battle rages forth.

The Kingdom

Simon MacCulloch

We serve an older power than the priests
Whose pallid wine-plunged wafers recollect
The ritualistic passion of our feasts.

Before they even learned to stand erect
Your ancestors would snuffle at the gore
In which profane and sacred intersect:

Profane, the drooling hunger, at whose core
The fangs of brute survival snap and bite,
The talons of possession snatch and claw;

Yet sacred, in the mystical delight
Of self-expansion, opening the eye
That holds the cosmos writhing in its sight.

So when at last, the well of life drained dry,
We wither in the oven of the sun,
A god will rise from where our ashes lie.
For we have pledged allegiance to the one
Whose will has been embodied in the beasts;
In Heaven as on Earth it shall be done.

Ratatoskr

Christian Dickinson

"Oh my—what plumage! What divine wingspan!
I don't believe you're molting in the least!
Oh, what—who said? That filthy, Hel-bound beast?
Well, I don't know—I swear it, by Wotan!"

"Heil Þú, my dear—how keep our fair trees' roots?
Your scales don't look at all like brittle clay!
Wait, what—Hræsvelgr? Now, I can't quite say . . .
One hears such rumors on these long commutes."

So up and down, then up and down I go,
To take my news from root to canopy.
And as I run, such dainty gossip hear,
Which pour I into each the other's ear—
For by this trick, I keep a living tree,
And save myself from boredom's hammer-blow.

ghosts in trees

Lori R. Lopez

There are shadows among the branches . . .
shaped like people perched on boughs, huddled
as if dark brooding birds. A morbid murder, a cult
of clamoring complaining crows. Spooky doves
squatting in patches of sinister pallid moonlight.
Why do only I view them, aware of the scrutiny?

How long have they been plotting, judging, spying?
I see them everywhere: ghosts in trees. Dismal
haunting figures. Looming, crouching, waiting . . .
Dim silhouettes, tenebral impressions. Somber,
opaque. Clumps of gloomy apparitions with deep
abiding stares. Resembling oversized owls.

Hunched like Old People. Spectral, kind of weird;
seated along limbs, a little obsessed. Observing me
while I gander them in hasty furtive indirect glances—
unsettled by the candor of lofty gazes. Cringing;
gooseflesh prickling under the weight and intensity
of a searing focus. What *are* they if not imagined?

A gathering of watchers? A crop of nuts and fruits?
Is there nothing else to occupy or divert them, claim
their unspoken fascination? What could they seek
from this creepy constant vigil? Why did they choose

my life to examine? No clues can be found delving
mental boxes, internal drawers of secrets . . .

Private failings, losses, woes. I glean naught
that might explain, even less excuse their passive
yet aggressive stares and interest. Nor have I heard
of others suffering this fate. It cannot be reserved for
me alone! I refuse to be the solitary object of their
wrath, target of their collective attentive blame.

A receptacle of scorn and misery. I reject their
disdain! Ignorance is not the same as innocence,
I know. But I deserve to be told the reason for such
blank condemnation—what led to such devoted
absorption—what drove these revenants to assemble
as sentinels of sorrow. In the arms of Weeping Willows.

Have I gone completely mad? Perhaps it isn't me at all
but a cosmic warning . . . an arcane statement from
the Universe, and I the humble Translator-Prophet-Poet,
or plagued Middle-Messenger. Could it be a silent Omen,
forecast of Doom? A less obvious revelation, symptom
or signal of impending Cataclysm; an Apocalypse?

Too late, drowned by the cries of Science, modern
Harbingers. Climates grown dire on a planet spinning

in a downward spiral. The earth so cluttered with animal
corpses and souls, human spirits must inhabit what trees
withstand the gales, catastrophic heat, storms and droughts,
as floods soak the sheets of homeless wraiths . . .

Perhaps they have simply accumulated to glimpse
the last Curtain Call. An audience for the Grand Finale.
Everyone loves a spectacle. Maybe I am merely the first
to gaze back! Reflect their rapt solemnity; that grave
contemplation and reverie. I might be the only
survivor to look up and notice—there's a crowd.

To Haunt Ancestral Tombs

Adam Bolivar

I wandered in a wood one morn
To haunt ancestral tombs,
And found them overgrown with thorn
Bereft of vibrant blooms.

The stones were in a shameful state,
Inscriptions badly worn,
And I was left to mull my fate,
My skin incised by thorn.

One name at least I could make out,
My kith from long ago;
That I was there I had no doubt
The dead must surely know.

A drop of blood from injured skin
Upon the stone then fell,
Enough to satisfy my kin,
Who hungered long in Hell.

Through broken bricks I spied a gap,
A space to crawl inside,
And let Death's arms around me wrap
My pale sepulchral bride.

Instead I mustered all my will
To flee that cursèd place,
Though in my bones I bore a chill,
And marks upon my face.

Fogs of Judgment

Janice Klain

Particles rising from the murk, floating around us,
vying to form into a being not unlike you or me;
Droplets of grayish matter desperately yearning to morph to the human dimension.

Whirling, waiting, praying for an opening to make a move into our awareness,
seeping in to our personal space,
Mocking, joking, playing mind games so everything unwittingly appears the same.

Hollow, transparent, opaque, a being, a specter
ready to embody our expanse,
Mimicking our moves and thoughts, converging into a world it can never survive.

Be on guard! . . .
The fog hides many a lifeform ready to become a shred of one's self.

Through Sunset's Gates

David Barker

Near end of day I gaze out to the west:
The town revealed more rich than I would say
When walking down its lanes at bright midday.
Faint crimson rays unmask its secrets best.
At sunset in the frigid wintertime
Lost memories escape their ancient vault,
Like arrows pierce my heart in quick assault,
And whisk my soul off to a sultry clime.

While there I revel in a world now gone,
Commune with friends now parted from this life,
And live again days free of grief and strife,
But only for an instant, then move on.
For that's a land where we may never stay,
But only glimpse at fleeting close of day.

Inspired by H. P. Lovecraft's sonnet "XIII. Hesperia" in *Fungi from Yuggoth*.

Young Friend

William Clunie

Do you recall the bloody spires
of Illyrium? The council of the dead?
Do you remember all the times
we stole a cup of wine and fled
to hellscapes of eternal night,
a crimson moon above our head?

I wonder what's become of you,
dead now, if you're in some other hell
of whistling pipes and broken shells
of short-lived folk, who shamble
through their dull pedestrian doom.

Arkham Boys' Summer Afternoon

David C. Kopaska-Merkel

The rails have been recycled
timbers rolled aside
this flat-topped ridge
ends at a tumble of weathered boards
behind, barbed wire sags in the dirt
between beetle-gnawed posts
leaning in or out
oaks and hickories
shoulder aside pitted limestone slabs
that gape like rotten teeth
all carving long effaced
small creatures scuttle through
brown curled leaves
any skeletal hands
that once reached heavenward
long since snapped off
in sharp-toothed jaws
wizards once interred here
perhaps to rise again
have shot their wads
a box turtle sticks out its head
eldritch as it gets

Fade

Lee Clark Zumpe

The silt of passing decades
falls in mounting layers,
blanketing the fading memories
of eternal youth.

I swim through centuries
under the watchful eyes
of a billion distant suns
brushing off the sediment.

The authors of my genesis
cower in nocturnal lairs,
retiring from flames
that radiate darkness visible.

And in some vespertine cavern
in the vast abyss of time,
your hungry soul lies waiting:
I fade into eternity.

Cosmic Mind

Ron L. Johnson II

Teleport anywhere in this or the next spacetime.
Just by way of cosmic-electromagnetic thought,
Become the Martian Dust Devil's holly grime.
Be the one who can't be deleted or divinely bought.

Become the lycanthrope matriarch with jagged canines stained.
Be the bots that gradually realized their own malicious minds.
Become a sabertoothed cat with a fungal bioluminescent mane.
Transport to a realm that droningly and deeply chimes.

Form a phantom-vortex of phosphorescent space-dust intertwined.
Be an interdimensional warlock that can cause dissolving acid rain.
Become a White Wormhole that slithers with Cosmic Serpentines.
Formulate a spectral star that lives to explode beings in vain.
When the mind dies, the body is consumed in a blazing force-flame.
Be the energy that Phoenix rises into another realm that sustains.

Bedeviled Kiss

Ashley Dioses

His mouth is sealed in runes
By my bedeviled kiss.
His heart beats fast to tunes
That in his ears I hiss.

He sails upon my waves
And comes whenever I
Allure him, for he craves
My salt, my winds, my cry.

No siren song's as fierce
As my swift, howling gales.
No mermaid's kiss can pierce
His love for my tall tales.

No selkie skin can shine
Like my bedazzled tides.
No kelpie is as fine
As my soft sandy sides.

And yet his death is near;
For me, he gives his life
To sail across seas clear
Of burdens, pain, and strife.

He gives in unto to me,
And ever I await
For his descent to sea
To meet his timely fate.

Eager Pupil

Katherine Kerestman

Magister, teach me. I burn to learn.
Flames leap in my core,
Fire rages in my veins,
I am alight.
Cool my desire with nightmare whispers from your lips.

Magister, teach me loathsome secrets,
Nightmare knowledge from dank
Charnel soil, miserable blasphemies out of
Forgotten catacombs
Tenant abandoned.

Magister, teach me. In a black cauldron glowing red
Meld two into one
Hideous thing. The incantation
Graven in your mind,
Teach it me, Magister.

A Colossus in Dream

Maxwell I. Gold

Through the shadow and mist I saw the manifold beast, so grotesque as it swayed in the foam and fog, this wanton harbinger swathed by seaweed, rock, and bones. *Come, terry to the water,* came the godless words through syrupy lips that smacked above me as if the oceans themselves had congealed with slime. Below me the feet of a man, huge and hideous, pressed deeper into the bedrock, sinking toward the tired nothingness; whereupon my consciousness gave way to the terrible and colossal figure who loomed like some dreadful expectation unable to be reached.

Closer I found myself waltzing to the bizarre, twisted muck-song that spilled from wide, crooked jaws whose teeth cut the clouds and splintered the vaults that were otherwise unbreakable, and the stars fell ne'er to reach the colossus' brow. Unthinkable were the possibilities that broke upon the shores of my brain, back and forth, *come, terry to the water,* they said as I cowered in the dank shade that grew heavy and slick with odor of rust and metal.

All at once, low and tedious came a profuse baritone chuckle through crooked streams, and salty tears as I met the empty eyes of a Promethean monster; a colossus who'd waited for thirteen billion years to carry me away to those dreadful waters.

Emperor Julian in the Afterworld

Darrell Schweitzer

He was never deified.
His successors, Christians all,
called him merely "apostate."
Yet he had served the gods so faithfully
and with such ardor
that surely he must have made it to Olympus on his own.

The journey would have been long and hard,
but in the end did he get there
only to find the thrones empty?
Did he himself sit in the very seat of Zeus,
hold the useless thunderbolt and scepter
in his hands, and gaze down
upon a darkening world?

If so, he must have done it
with such tragic and heroic dignity
that his last sigh sounded
like the final note of an exquisite,
mournful hymn
even as his shadow faded
and the dust stirred by his passage
was finally still.

Among the Trees

F. J. Bergmann

Nature is all well and good,
the lush greenery growing
ever denser, birds crying out
warnings as you approach
that are passed onward,
small rustlings & chitterings
from animals you never see,
dappled light going gold,
a cool mist thickening,
but what prickles your spine
is the dark exhalation from
that hole between the roots,
those stairs going down.

What They Say

Ngo Binh Anh Khoa

They say I am the Devil's slave,
A hideous crone, a wicked knave;
Their toxic tongues would wag and curse
To see whose insult bites the worst.

(But those same clowns that preach and taunt
Would creep in shadow's cloak to haunt
My hut and beg for favors dark;
How docilely those mutts then bark.)

They say I am a monstrous blight
That preys on innocent souls at night;
Their eyes shine with self-righteous scorn
As their mouths spout words wrapped in thorns.

(But those same eyes would starkly gleam
With hoards of predatory dreams:
Luck, power, wealth, eternal youth—
Each one reveals a rotten truth.)

They say I am a venomous snake
That leaves but misery in its wake;
How their teeth grind and nostrils flare
As hate erupts from scorching glares.

(But those same pearly teeth would smile
At herbs and potions, cruel and vile,
At charms and hexes meant to kill
Or rob a person of their will.)

They say I am an ominous wench
Enshrouded in Death's horrid stench,
A heap of dung that plagues their town,
Whose sinful soul for Hell is bound.

(But those same buzzing pests would swarm
My hut like flies, as is their norm,
For spells to glean things from the dead;
Soon, breaths are stilled, and blood is shed.)

They say I am a wretched stain
Behind my back time and again;
Their faces twist, deformed by rage
As they shout from their lofty stage.

(But those cracked masks can't hide their cores
As they crawl back to me for more—
More deals, more favors at all costs;
To Heaven, hence, their souls are lost.)

Hypercathexis to a Sunken Spell

Manuel Pérez-Campos

Beneath waves of azureous semi-transparent roar
just off a cove's curve where palm trees are taking
command of the dusk's west wind, and where dirt
and rocks move like brute notes in slow flows
unending amid a briny carnival of slugs and conches
in plurivalent copulas, current-fluffed and -lifted medusas
of gangly shapeshifter cunning, those adepts
of fluid mechanics that itch to riffle a mariner
in their labyrinthine streamers and capable of perfect
dissolutions into ambient shade disseminate
as though an invasion of lurkers which resemble
phantasmatic blossoms of fiery vibe-sensitive
complexity throughout a numinous vent-fed basin.
Avaunt, O marauders of mesopelagic incognito!
Summon no more through psychic insistence one
whose grotesque prehuman predecessors,
those lethargic lobe-finned fish part of whose
double helix twist still shapes with feeble but insidious
tenacity my inner organs opted out of the agony of
being feasted on with gelatinous diligence
by thy frigid clan—lest in secret I resume
their envying the aromatized razzmatazz of thy tremored
coilings and chamberings until phylogenetic memory

activates an overarching necessity to inhale
the green abyss—and a maroon starfish, the ridges
on its pentaradial arms like heatstruck hieroglyphs,
lodge behind my ribs as I decay, my hair stained a deep
pink by algae, and oversee my coronation by barnacles.

Walker of Wastes

Scott J. Couturier

A white thing walks amid pale drifts of snow—
Shambling slow, as a being newly dead
& returned to unlikely life must go.

Effigy of hunger, it wanders wastes by night—
Ghastly wight from out grave's bourne,
Cloaked in ice, monstrance of fright.

Devoid of blood to bleed, yet on blood it feeds—
Overtaking many a lonesome wanderer far,
With fang & claw it satiates its needs.

Some mistake it for a vagrant in want of aid—
Thus it lures with pity, cheating charity,
A wanton & revulsive charade.

Others it summons in a lost lover's voice—
Cries risen from blizzard's darkness,
Prey given a torturous choice.

Oft it climbs into boughs of ancient pine—
Waiting with ravenous lust to strike,
Like a starveling babe it whines.

Undead lurker, haunter, exemplar of winter—
Weird outline of skulking, savage form,

A horror Death itself disinterred.
Ware this wan walker clad in corpse's shroud—
Heed no word from swamp or wood,
Nor an infant's wailing loud:

For it will come to no good.

In a Garden of Hounds

Benjamin Blake

The silent call of the oak grove
Rang out in my skull.
The branches that danced overhead,
Spilled rays of celestial light
Through frost-kissed fingertips.
A blessing, unexpected and ineffable.

I had stood in the same spot years before,
In a time before the world
Had given up what sanity it possessed.

The future hangs uncertain,
But there are ancient signs
That need no interpretation.
And something gloriously fierce
Is waiting
To do as it will.

On the Himalayas of Nicholas Roerich's Series of Paintings

Manuel Pérez-Campos

It is a high country where peaks self-replicate
perfervidly as though possessed by a titanic desire
to be immortal: where the massive subfusc gate
of an eclipse-hid lamasery almost entrenched
in invisibility lets in abominable shamblers
of snowflake wisdom whose white fur is drenched
in the fugitive opalescence of a sunset's fire
and where slabs scattered around its perimeter
wear the deep scars of ages of erosion by gales
that hurl travellers into unretrievable emptinesses.
O thou who peerest from afar with the hauteur
of one estranged from the lucidly swirled traces
of sky-annexed paths left by his brush: this is thy curse:
to be repelled by these symbolic hardships and travails:
and not to be able to live within this near-intransitable
realm that depicts a forgotten yearning of thy soul.

Classic Reprints

Midnight

Archibald Lampman

From where I sit, I see the stars,
    And down the chilly floor
The moon between the frozen bars
    Is glimmering dim and hoar.

Without in many a peakèd mound
    The glinting snowdrifts lie;
There is no voice or living sound;
    The embers slowly die.

Yet some wild thing is in mine ear;
    I hold my breath and hark;
Out of the depth I seem to hear
    A crying in the dark:

No sound of man or wife or child,
    No sound of beast that groans,
Or of the wind that whistles wild,
    Or of the tree that moans:

I know not what it is I hear;
    I bend my head and hark:
I cannot drive it from mine ear,
    That crying in the dark.

[From Archibald Lampman (1861–1899), *Among the Millet and Other Poems* (Ottowa: J. Durie & Son, 1888).]

Adam to Lilith

E. Hoffmann Price

And now, in these my uneventful days
When life assumes a dreary, sallow glaze,
And pallid virtue's leprous hue
Sickens and wearies me, I think of you
Who lured me to your silken lupanar,
Perfumed with musk and purple nenuphar,
An afreet's cavern on an eastern isle,
A darkness lumined by your hyacinthine smile. . . .
Lilith, the twining midnight of your hair
Across my wandering path has laid a snare,
A coiling maze of subtle witchery
That binds and traps me irresistibly.

[First published in *Weird Tales* 7, No. 1 (January 1926): 59.]

Reviews

Fireside Poems

Kyla Lee Ward

COLLEEN ANDERSON. *Weird Worlds*. Introduction by Marge Simon. Central Point, OR: Weird House Press, 2024. xv, 127 pp. $14.99 tpb.

It is good to read some poetry that is actually weird, rather than simply weird poetry! And this is a substantial body of work. As Anderson's 2023 collection *The Lore of Inscrutable Dreams* explored the secret life of objects, so this volume delves into organs, bones and teeth, hair and nails, frequently as discrete entities. As bodies approach their limits, terrible and gorgeous things occur.

An Aztec priest addresses impassioned words to the sacrifice in "Bloodthirst." The lover coming heart in hand is a charming metaphor, that has a rather different impact in the flesh. But then the reader may wish to contemplate "The Drowning Ones," where the bodies and minds of the chosen are prepared from birth for their eventual fate, introduced to the water a toe at a time.

> No acolyte knows for sure, but Drowning Ones are taught to lift their legs spread to the ocean, let it enter them entirely, being one.

In "The Apprentice," a student devoted to their sorcerous master is reshaped in a manner exquisitely fitting, though hardly what they had in mind. But the transformation of lovers in "Wolfskin" is desire triumphant, a grisly climax of passion transcending any single physical shape. This may also be a metaphor, but I doubt they care.

"The Metallurgist's Dream" sees another lover flex their craft rather than their claws, attempting to transcend death.

> into the crucible I place your parts
> melt everything for your essence
> your iron will and quicksilver pulse
> that mercurial mind that fired you . . .

This may be overreaching, and the magician the reader encounters at the "Crossroads" knows full well what price may be exacted for such hubris. But the dying visionary of "Divinity in the Afterglow" forges hope from materials equally inert.

The breadth of vision and craft that is showcased in this collection is astonishing but not surprising: Colleen Anderson is one of the most accomplished poets working in the field today. Her grasp of how to make free verse work as poetry is masterly, generating rhythm and form through the cadences of speech, and a style reminiscent of fireside tale-telling that is nonetheless distinctly hers. There are also traditional forms herein, pyramidal tercets building and dismantling meaning, and the piece titled "Upon Discovery," which is both a word palindrome and spectacular concrete poetry.

The brain may enjoy being stretched by unfamiliar perspectives, subverted expectations, and some truly surreal imagery. Other parts of the reader's body may be disturbed or even queasy (let us hope not rebellious). But as this kind of sheer, visceral response is a rarity in poetry of any sort, it deserves to be celebrated, as Anderson's *Weird Worlds* deserves to be read. Come revel in all the grotesque glory of bodies deconstructed, constructs embodied, and the dust that was once entire civilizations.

Halloween Redux

S. T. Joshi

K. A. OPPERMAN. *October Ghosts and Autumn Dreams: More Poems for Halloween.* Foreword by Adam Bolivar. [Salem, OR]: Jackanapes Press, 2021. 118 pp. $14.99 tpb.
K. A. OPPERMAN. *At Wistful Summer's End: Last Poems for Halloween.* [Salem, OR]: Jackanapes Press, 2024. 121 pp. $15.99 tpb.

It has been nearly a decade since K. A. Opperman burst onto the weird poetry scene with *The Crimson Tome* (Hippocampus Press, 2015), a scintillating volume that displayed to the full not merely the author's metrical deftness but also the powerful horrific imagination that infuses every one of his poems. Since then, Opperman has published several additional poetry collections—*Past the Sunlit Season: Poems for Halloween* (Jackanapes Press, 2020), *The Laughter of Ghouls* (Hippocampus Press, 2021), and the two volumes reviewed here.

October Ghosts and Autumn Dreams is one more book of Halloween poems. The fact that Opperman was able to produce another volume on the subject was something of a surprise to the author himself, who notes in his introduction, "I never planned to write a second book of Halloween poems, but as with the first book, I just kept writing them, and writing them, and soon, one thing led to another." Opperman was wise to follow his poetic instincts, for this second book rings a remarkable number of changes on what might appear to be a limited set of motifs—the mystery of pumpkins, the rituals of Halloween (trick-or-treating, bobbing for apples), the magic of autumn, and so on. One poem piquantly envisions a "cat-o'-lantern" (a pumpkin carved in the likeness of a cat), with baleful results: "A grinning, fanged, grimalkin moon / Soon rose, invoked by yowling cry, / And like a draping crepe festoon— / A chain of witches crossed the sky."

In "The Three Pretty Pumpkins," one of the longer poems in the book, three "pumpkin sprites" come to life, wreaking havoc on the hapless human beings they encounter. So too, in another poem, a "pumpkin maiden" gains anomalous life, but her end is not a happy one: "At last the dawn, a cosmic marigold, / Began to blossom from behind the hill, / But as the world awoke, she fell so still— / Her squashy body crumbling unto mold." That metaphor of the sun as a "cosmic marigold" is an imperishable image.

Opperman is particularly sensitive to the change of season from summer to autumn, and "Sunflowers" captures this transition hauntingly: "With burnt and blackened faces, withered crowns, / The nodding liches watch their season's death; / The leaves that turn to yellows, reds, and browns, / Blown o'er the lawns as by a witch's breath." So, too, does "The Season" speak broodingly of time and change: "This is the autumn, when the moon / Soars mournfully beyond our reach— / When distant owls sadly croon / A tragic, secret truth to teach." The book's theme is perhaps summed up in a poem that is placed close to the end: "Amidst the bleak advances of November, / There is a hollow lost in hidden dells— / A secret place I always will remember, / Where yet October dwells."

October Ghosts and Autumn Dreams concludes with an afterword and perhaps excessively lengthy "poem notes." But whether writing poetry or prose, Opperman rings the bell over and over, in verse of meticulous precision, lyrical beauty, and wondrously evocative imagery.

Opperman's most recent volume, *At Summer's Wistful End*, purports to be the poet's "last" book of Halloween poems. Surely, by this time, the poet has at last reached a point where he is simply restating what he has said before! But no: the author manages to generate still more variations on his cherished themes. This time he urges us to see how Halloween comes inexorably upon us in the months preceding; the advent of the fateful month is unmistakable: "October is coming, so say your goodbyes / To youth and to yesterday's glow. / The crows are a-circling on violet skies, / And leaves toward oblivion blow." There is a place, it appears, called Pumpkin Creek ("far, yet near"), and it allows us to know that "Halloween is almost here." There is also something called Devil's Night, "When ravens flee in sunset flight, / And briefly form a haunting night— / A devil newly woke."

Halloween is populated by owls, black cats, and other creatures who bring menace and fear to one and all. Even inanimate things such as dead leaves are full of foreboding: "Dead leaves remind me of what was, / And what shall never be again— / Time blows away, it always does, / Days lost like leaves in yonder glen." And what are we to make of the ambiguous entity that is the focus of "Black Laurels"?—"I will be known unto the witch, / And all of her nocturnal kin— / In life, though neither loved, nor rich, / In death black laurels will I win."

Opperman's trilogy of Halloween poems is a notable achievement in weird verse. For all their seemingly repetitive focus on a relatively limited number of subjects and motifs, the poet consistently surprises us with distinctive images and perspectives that make each poem fresh and vital. And it cannot be emphasized too forcefully that the layout of the two books under review, generously illustrated by the publisher, Dan Sauer, significantly augments the shuddersome pleasure of reading them. A more felicitous union of memorable poetry and vivid artwork would be difficult to find in contemporary literature.

Notes on Contributors

Adam Amberden is a human being currently residing on the planet Earth. Possessed of adequate proficiency in the written form of the English language, he sometimes uses this aptitude to produce poetry reflective of his existential dread. Other humans have, at times, described him as "weird." His first published work appeared in *Spectral Realms* 21.

Manuel Arenas is a writer of verse and prose in the Gothic Horror tradition. His work has appeared in various anthologies and journals including *Spectral Realms* and *Penumbra* (both from Hippocampus Press) and *Weird Fiction Quarterly* (Alien Sun Press). He has two collections of prose and poetry, available from Jackanapes Press: *Book of Shadows* (2021) and *The Burning Ember Mission of Helldorado* (2024).

David Barker has been writing weird fiction and poetry since the mid-1980s. His horror story collection *Her Wan Embrace* appeared in 2019, followed by *12 Foot Skeleton Halloween Poems* in 2023. David's work has appeared in many magazines and anthologies including *Fungi*, *Cyäegha*, *Weird Fiction Review*, *The Audient Void*, *Nightmare's Realm*, *Forbidden Knowledge*, *Spectral Realms*, *The Art Mephitic*, *A Walk in a Darker Wood*, and *A Walk in a City of Shadows*.

F. J. Bergmann edits poetry for *Mobius: The Journal of Social Change* and imagines tragedies on or near exoplanets. His work appears irregularly in *Analog*, *Asimov's*, *Polu Texni*, *Pulp Literature*, *Silver Blade*, and elsewhere. A *Catalogue of the Further Suns*, a collection of dystopian first-contact poems, won the 2017 Gold Line Press poetry chapbook contest and is available at fibitz.com.

Benjamin Blake is the author of the novel *The Devil's Children* and the poetry collections *Standing on the Threshold of Madness, Southpaw Nights* (poetry & prose), *All the Feral Dogs of Los Angeles* (with Cole Bauer), *Dime Store Poetry,* and *Tenebrae in Aeternum* (Hippocampus Press, 2020). He lives in the South West of England.

Adam Bolivar is a poet and writer of weird and folkloric fantasy, as well as a playwright for marionettes. He is the author of *The Lay of Old Hex* (Hippocampus Press, 2017), *The Ettinfell of Beacon Hill* (Jackanapes Press, 2021), *Ballads for the Witching Hour* (Hippocampus Press, 2022), and *A Wheel of Ravens* (Jackanapes Press, 2023). A native of gambrel-roofed Boston, Massachusetts, he now resides in the gloomy dreamlands of Portland, Oregon.

William Clunie is an American poet living in Berlin. His work has appeared in *Dreams and Nightmares, Star*Line,* and as a collection from Demain Publishing, *Laws of Discord.* He would like to think his primary influences are Shakespeare, Milton, and Poe. He is married to a German woman named Sandra. They are quite happy together.

Frank Coffman is a retired professor of college English, creative writing, and journalism. He has published speculative poetry and fiction in a variety of journals, magazines, and anthologies. His fourth large collection of speculative verse, *What the Night Brings,* was published in August 2023. A collection of his short fiction, *Maxime Miris: 15 Tales of the Weird, Horrific, and Supernatural,* is forthcoming. Writing formal poetry in the *Weird Tales* tradition is his mission.

Scott J. Couturier is a Rhysling Award–nominated poet and prose writer of the weird, liminal, and darkly fantastic. His work has appeared in numerous venues, including *The Audient Void, Spectral Realms, Tales from the Magician's Skull, Space and Time Magazine, Cosmic Horror Monthly,* and *Weirdbook*; his collection of weird fiction, *The Box,* is available from

Hybrid Sequence Media, while his collection of autumnal & folk horror verse, *I Awaken in October*, is available from Jackanapes Press.

Christian Dickinson is an Assistant Professor of English Literature at Brewton-Parker College in Mount Vernon, Georgia. Besides teaching, Dr. Dickinson's great passion is for writing; while his scholarly work analyzes the intersection of religion and literature of the nineteenth century, his creative work operates in the realm of the speculative and fantastic. To date he has had the blessing to publish sixteen poems about creatures from a variety of cultural myths.

Ashley Dioses is a writer of dark poetry and fiction from southern California. Her debut collection of dark traditional poetry, *Diary of a Sorceress*, was published in 2017 by Hippocampus Press. Jackanapes Press has published two collections of her early works, *The Withering* and *Darkest Days and Haunted Ways*. A new collection, *Diary of a Vampyress*, is forthcoming.

Under the pseudonym **J. D. Dresner,** Jared Reid writes wildly illustrative poetry and short stories that often follow an unusual and unpredictable format. When Dresner isn't developing new spells within his poetry sanctum, he is brewing up new fiction from his cauldron of lies. He lives in Maple Ridge, British Columbia, Canada, where he provides professional layout, design, and editorial work for small book publishers.

Ian Futter began writing stories and poems in his childhood, but only lately has started to share them. One of his poems appears in *The Darke Phantastique* (Cycatrix Press, 2014), and he continues to produce dark fiction for admirers of the surreal.

Joshua Gage is an ornery curmudgeon from Cleveland. He currently co-edits the horror poetry journal *Otoroshi Journal* with his life partner, Rowan Beckett. His newest chapbook, *blips on a screen*, is available on Cuttlefish Books. He is a graduate of the Low Residency MFA Program in Creative Writing at Naropa University. He has a penchant for Pendleton shirts, Ethiopian coffee, and any poem strong enough to yank the breath out of his lungs.

Adele Gardner's poetry collection *Halloween Hearts* is available from Jackanapes Press. With poems and stories in *Analog, Clarkesworld, Strange Horizons, Daily Science Fiction,* and more, Adele curated the 2019 SFPA Halloween Poetry Reading and serves as literary executor for father, mentor, and namesake Delbert R. Gardner.

Wade German's most recent full-length poetry collection is *Psalms and Sorceries* (Hippocampus Press, 2022). His first collection, *Dreams from a Black Nebula,* is also available from Hippocampus Press. Other titles include four slim volumes of his selected poems with Portuguese translation: *Incantations, Apparitions, Phantasmagorias,* and the latest, *Chapel of Celluloid* (Raphus Press, 2023).

Maxwell I. Gold is a Jewish-American multiple award-nominated author who writes prose poetry and short stories in cosmic horror and weird fiction with half a decade of writing experience. He is a five-time Rhysling Award nominee and two-time Pushcart Award nominee.

Joshua Green is a speculative fiction author whose work has been translated into more than seven languages. He writes for Studio Midhall, a board game company based in Malmö, Sweden, where he creates engaging stories within the Beast universe. He is a full member of the Science Fiction and Fantasy Writers Association and lives in northern Minnesota with his wife, three children, and the ever-eccentric mini-Aussie named Juni.

Jay Hardy is an artist, editor, and poet from knee deep in the heart of Louisiana's Cajun Country. He is a lifelong fan of "The Alphabet Boys": HPL, REH, ERB, and CAS. His poetry is either weirdly humorous or humorously weird. His poems have appeared in *Ellery Queen's Mystery*

Magazine and the *Hyborian Gazette*. He has self-published several poetry collections, including *Always Eleven: Poems Inspired by Stranger Things, My Mommy Hates Halloween, Living Longmire, Cats of Cairo*, and *The Paranoid Pirate*.

Ron L. Johnson II graduated from Webster University with a B.A. in Photography. Since digitalization has put film on the endangered list, he writes now with words instead of light. Ron has had poems published in numerous issues of *Spectral Realms*. He has also had an article on "The Dunwich Horror" and *Ghostbusters* published in the *Lovecraft Annual* No. 17 (2023).

Katherine Kerestman is the author of *Lethal* (PsychoToxin Press, 2023), *Creepy Cat's Macabre Travels* (WordCrafts Press, 2020), and *Haunted Houses and Other Strange Tales* (Hippocampus Press, 2024), as well as the co-editor (with S. T. Joshi) of *The Weird Cat* (WordCrafts Press, 2023) and *Shunned Houses* (Wordcrafts Press, 2024). Her Lovecraftian and gothic works have been featured in *Black Wings VII, Penumbra, Journ-E, Spectral Realms, Illumen, Retro-Fan, Dissections, Off-Course, Lovecraftiana* and other discerning publications.

With a background in the arts (non-dark), customer service and administration, travel, and tourism, and education, **Janice Klain** has plenty of experiences to draw from as she journeys through the world of the written word.

David C. Kopaska-Merkel won the 2006 Rhysling Award for best long poem (for a collaboration with Kendall Evans), and edits *Dreams & Nightmares* magazine (since 1986). He has edited *Star*Line* and several *Rhysling* anthologies. His poems have been published in *Asimov's, Analog, Strange Horizons*, and elsewhere. His latest collection, *Some Disassembly Required*, winner of the 2023 Elgin Award, was published by Diminuendo Press in 2022.

Lori R. Lopez is a quirky author, illustrator, poet, and songwriter who likes to wear hats. Her Gothic-toned and extensive poetry collection *Darkverse: The Shadow Hours* was nominated for the 2018 Elgin Award, while individual poems have been nominated for Rhysling Awards. Stories and verse appear in numerous publications. Other titles include *The Dark Mister Snark, Leery Lane, Odds & Ends, The room at the end of the hall, Cryptic Consequences,* and *An Ill Wind Blows.*

Simon MacCulloch once had a poem rejected by the *British Journal of Psychiatry* on grounds of bad taste. Not many people can say that.

C. R. Molœny is an Anglo-Irish American fictioneer, poet, playwright, and amateur pressman. He has a special affinity for prose-poetry and the weaving of cycles. His work does not belong to a singular genre, though oftentimes leans towards the preternatural and the mediæval. Apart from college journals, this is his first worldly appearance. He is a native of Long Island.

D. L. Myers is a dark poet from the Pacific Northwest. His work has appeared in *Spectral Realms, Eye to the Telescope, The Audient Void, Black Wings VI, The 2020 Rhysling Anthology, Test Patterns,* and *A Walk in a Darker Wood.* His first collection, *Oracles from the Black Pool,* was published by Hippocampus Press in 2019.

Kurt Newton's poetry has appeared in numerous magazines and anthologies. He is the author of eight collections of poetry. His ninth collection, *Songs of the Underland and Other Macabre Machinations,* was recently published by Ravens Quoth Press.

Ngo Binh Anh Khoa is a teacher of English in Ho Chi Minh City, Vietnam. In his free time, he enjoys daydreaming, reading, and occasionally writing poetry for personal entertainment. His speculative poems have appeared in NewMyths.com, *Heroic Fantasy Quarterly, The Audient Void,* and other venues.

Manuel Pérez-Campos's poetry has appeared previously in *Spectral Realms* and *Weird Fiction Review*. A collection of his poetry in the key of the weird is in progress; so is a collection of ground-breaking essays on H. P. Lovecraft. He lives in Bayamón, Puerto Rico.

Michael Potts is the author of three novels: *End of Summer*, *Unpardonable Sin*, and *Obedience*, all published by WordCrafts Press. He also has published three volumes of poetry: *From Field to Thicket* (winner, 2006 Mary Belle Campbell Poetry Book Award, North Carolina Writers Network), *Hiding from the Reaper and Other Horror Poems*, and *Slipknot and Other Dark Poems*. He serves as Professor of Philosophy, Methodist University, Fayetteville, North Carolina.

Carl E. Reed is employed as the showroom manager for a window, siding, and door company just outside Chicago. Former jobs include U.S. marine, long-haul trucker, improvisational actor, cab driver, security guard, bus driver, door-to-door encyclopedia salesman, construction worker, and art show MC. His poetry has been published in the *Iconoclast* and *Spectral Realms*; short stories in *Black Gate* and *newWitch* magazines.

Geoffrey Reiter is Associate Professor and Coordinator of Literature at Lancaster Bible College. He is also an Associate Editor at the website *Christ and Pop Culture*, where he frequently writes about weird horror and dark fantasy. As a scholar of weird fiction, Reiter has published academic articles on such authors as Arthur Machen, Bram Stoker, Clark Ashton Smith, and William Peter Blatty. His poetry has previously appeared in *Spectral Realms* and *Star*Line*, and his fiction has appeared in *Penumbra* and *The Mythic Circle*.

Silvatiicus Riddle is a twice Rhysling Award–nominated dark fantasy and speculative fiction writer and poet. He studied English and Literature at Kingsborough. His poetry has appeared in *Abyss & Apex*, *Dreams & Nightmares*, *Enchanted Living*, *Eternal Haunted Summer*, and *Spectral Realms*. His fiction has appeared in *Apex Magazine*'s "Strange

Locations" anthology, and several issues of *Weird Fiction Quarterly*. His newsletter, *The Goblin's Reliquary*, focuses on utilizing fantasy, folklore, and myth to combat entropy and despair.

Ann K. Schwader lives and writes in Colorado. Her newest collection, Unquiet Stars, is now out from Weird House Press. Two of her earlier collections, *Wild Hunt of the Stars* (Sam's Dot, 2010) and *Dark Energies* (P'rea Press, 2015), were Bram Stoker Award Finalists. In 2018, she received the Science Fiction and Fantasy Poetry Association's Grand Master award. She is also a two-time Rhysling Award winner.

Darrell Schweitzer has been publishing weird or fantastic poetry for decades. Not counting comic verse (e.g., *They Never Found the Head: Poems of Sentiment and Reflection*, 2001) his two previous collections of (mostly weird) verse are *Groping Toward the Light* (2000) and *Ghosts of Past and Future* (2008). Hippocampus Press will issue a new volume of previously uncollected and selected poems, *Dancing Before Azathoth*, in 2025. His most recent story collection is *The Children of Chorazin* (Hippocampus, 2023) and his most recent anthology is *Shadows out of Time* (PS Publishing, 2023).

John Shirley won the Bram Stoker Award for his book *Black Butterflies: A Flock on the Dark Side*. His first poetry collection, *The Voice of the Burning House*, has been nominated for the Elgin Award for poetry.

Claire Smith writes about other worlds: fairy tale, folkloric, mythological, and more. Her work has featured in a number of journals and anthologies, including earlier editions of *Spectral Realms*, *Penumbric Speculative Fiction Magazine*, and *A Frolic of Fairies*. She is currently reading for a Ph.D. in English and Creative Writing at the University of Gloucestershire, specialising in Poetry. She lives in Gloucestershire, UK, with her husband, the writer, Oliver Smith and their very spoilt Tonkinese cat, Ishtar.

DJ Tyrer is the person behind Atlantean Publishing and has been published in *The 2016 Rhysling Anthology*, issues of *Cyäegha*, *The*

Horrorzine, Scifaikuest, Sirens Call, Star*Line, Tigershark, and *The Yellow Zine.* The e-chapbook *One Vision* is available from Tigershark Publishing. *SuperTrump* and *A Wuhan Whodunnit* are available for download from Atlantean Publishing.

Kyla Lee Ward is based in Sydney, Australia. She produces short fiction. articles and poetry, including Stoker and Rhysling Award nominees, and is co-author of the Aurealis Award-winning novel *Prismatic*. She is a founding member of Deadhouse Productions and a guide with the Rocks Ghost Tours. Her interests include history, occultism, and scaring innocent bystanders.

Andrew White lives like a monk in the mountains of North Carolina. He writes mystical poetry with elements of fantasy, mythology, and Gothic. Andrew loves nature, his family, and heavy metal. He has been published in *Spectral Realms, Dwarf Stars, Kali Yuga Rag, Great Tree Zen Temple,* and *Poetry Nation*.

Steven Withrow has written three chapbooks—*The Sun Ships, The Bedlam Philharmonic,* and *The Nothing Box*—and a collaborative collection, *The Exorcised Lyric* (with Frank Coffman). His speculative and dark fantasy poems have appeared in *Asimov's, Spectral Realms, Space & Time,* and *Dreams & Nightmares*. His work was nominated for the Rhysling and Elgin awards, and he wrote the libretto for a chamber opera based on a classic English ghost story. He lives on Cape Cod.

Lee Clark Zumpe, an entertainment editor with Tampa Bay Newspapers, earned his bachelor's degree in English at the University of South Florida. He began writing poetry and fiction in the early 1990s. His work has regularly appeared in a variety of literary journals and genre magazines over the last few decades.

www.ingramcontent.com/pod-product-compliance
Lightning Source LLC
Chambersburg PA
CBHW060810050426
42449CB00008B/1618